~A BINGO BOOK~

Famous People Bingo Book

COMPLETE BINGO GAME IN A BOOK

Written By Rebecca Stark

ON THE COVER

Center: Left to Right
William Clark and Meriwether Lewis

Clockwise: Starting on Top
Abraham Lincoln
Sacajawea
John Adams
Harriet Tubman
Paul Revere
Rosa Parks
James Madison

© Barbara M. Peller, also known as Rebecca Stark, 2016

The purchase of this book entitles the buyer to exclusive re-production rights of the student activity pages for his or her class only. The reproduction of any part of the work for an entire school or school system or for commercial use is prohibited.

ISBN 978-0-87386-457-2

Educational Books 'n' Bingo

Printed in the U.S.A.

FAMOUS PEOPLE BINGO DIRECTIONS

INCLUDED:

List of Terms

Templates for Additional Terms and Clues

2 Clues per Term

30 Unique Bingo Cards

Markers

1. **Either cut apart the book or make copies of ALL the sheets. You might want to make an extra copy of the clue sheets to use for introduction and review. Keep the sheets in an envelope for easy reuse.**

2. Cut apart the call cards with terms and clues.

3. Pass out one bingo card per student. There are enough for a class of 30.

4. Pass out markers. You may cut apart the markers included in this book or use any other small items of your choice.

5. Decide whether or not you will require the entire card to be filled. Requiring the entire card to be filled provides a better review. However, if you have a short time to fill, you may prefer to have them do the just the border or some other format. Tell the class before you begin what is required.

6. There are 50 terms. Read the list before you begin. If there are any terms that have not been covered in class, you may want to read to the students the term and clues before you begin.

7. There is a blank space in the middle of each card. You can instruct the students to use it as a free space or you can write in answers to cover terms not included. Of course, in this case you would create your own clues. (Templates provided.)

8. Shuffle the cards and place them in a pile. Two or three clues are provided for each term. If you plan to play the game with the same group more than once, you might want to choose a different clue for each game. If not, you may choose to use more than one clue.

9. Be sure to keep the cards you have used for the present game in a separate pile. When a student calls, "Bingo," he or she will have to verify that the correct answers are on his or her card AND that the markers were placed in response to the proper questions. Pull out the cards that are on the student's card keeping them in the order they were used in the game. Read each clue as it was given and ask the student to identify the correct answer from his or her card.

10. If the student has the correct answers on the card AND has shown that they were marked in response to the *correct questions,* then that student is the winner and the game is over. If the student does not have the correct answers on the card OR he or she marked the answers in response to *the wrong questions,* then the game continues until there is a proper winner.

11. If you want to play again, reshuffle the cards and begin again.

Have fun!

© Barbara M. Peller

PEOPLE

Abigail Adams

John Adams

Neil Armstrong

Susan B. Anthony

Clara Barton

Alexander Graham Bell

Ludwig van Beethoven

Christopher Columbus

Davy Crockett

Roald Dahl

Walt Disney

Frederick Douglass

Thomas Edison

Albert Einstein

Henry Ford

Benjamin Franklin

John Glenn

Jane Goodall

Nathan Hale

Alexander Hamilton

Patrick Henry

Henry Hudson

Thomas Jefferson

Helen Keller

Francis Scott Key

Martin Luther King, Jr.

Marquis de Lafayette

Robert E. Lee

Meriwether Lewis

Abraham Lincoln

James Madison

Ferdinand Magellan

James Monroe

Florence Nightingale

Barack Obama

Rosa Parks

Molly Pitcher

Pocahontas

Paul Revere

Betsy Ross

Sacajawea

Sequoyah

Dr. Seuss

William Shakespeare

Mark Twain

Harriet Tubman

Leonardo da Vinci

George Washington

Eli Whitney

Wright Brothers

© Barbara M. Peller

Additional People

Choose as many Famous People as you would like and write them in the squares. Repeat each as desired. Cut out the squares and randomly distribute them to the class. Instruct the students to place the square on the center space of their card.

Famous People Bingo

© Barbara M. Peller

Clues for Additional People

Write two or three clues for each of your Famous People.

_____ 1. 2. 3.	_____ 1. 2. 3.
_____ 1. 2. 3.	_____ 1. 2. 3.
_____ 1. 2. 3.	_____ 1. 2. 3.

© Barbara M. Peller

Abigail Adams

1. She was the wife of the first President and the mother of the sixth President.

2. This first lady wrote of the importance of women's rights in her letters to her husband. (Note: the term first lady was not yet used.)

John Adams

1. He was the first vice president and the second President of the United States.

2. His son later became the sixth President of the United States.

Neil Armstrong

1. In 1969 this astronaut became the first human to step on the moon.

2. When his foot touched the surface of the moon, he said "That's one small step for man; one giant leap for mankind."

Susan B. Anthony

1. She was among the founders of the National Woman Suffrage Association.

2. She and Elizabeth Cady Stanton were among those to attend the first American women's rights convention, held in Seneca Falls, NY, in 1848.

Clara Barton

1. She organized the American Red Cross.

2. She established an agency to get needed supplies to wounded soldiers during the American Civil War.

Alexander Graham Bell

1. He is credited with inventing the first practical telephone.

2. Best known for his invention of the telephone, this Scottish inventor was also a teacher of the deaf.

Ludwig van Beethoven

1. This great composer continued to compose even after he became deaf.

2. Two of the works of this great composer are his *Fifth Symphony* and *Moonlight Sonata.*

Christopher Columbus

1. When this explorer landed in the Bahamas in 1492, he thought he had found the East Indies.

2. Although he is usually credited with discovering America, America was named for Amerigo Vespucci.

Davy Crockett

1. This frontiersman became a folk hero, possibly because of the tall tales he liked to tell.

2. This frontiersman died defending the Alamo in Texas in 1836.

Roald Dahl

1. He is the author of *Charlie and the Chocolate Factory.*

2. He is author of *James and the Giant Peach.*

Famous People Bingo

© Barbara M. Peller

Walt Disney 1. He was the creator of Mickey Mouse. 2. His first children's theme park was built in California and opened in 1955.	**Frederick Douglass** 1. This great African-American abolitionist fought for women's suffrage as well as for abolition of slavery. 2. This African-American abolitionist and editor wrote an autobiography in 1845.
Thomas Edison 1. This inventor held a record 1,093 patents for his inventions. 2. Among his many inventions were the light bulb and the phonograph.	**Albert Einstein** 1. This German scientist is best known for his theory of relativity. Many people believe he was one of the smartest people ever. 2. His name is sometimes used when referring to a very smart person.
Henry Ford 1. Although he did not actually invent the automobile, his institution of the assembly line made it possible for more people to afford one. 2. His company's Model T is regarded as the first affordable automobile.	**Benjamin Franklin** 1. He was born in Boston but made his home in Philadelphia. He was never President, but he was one of the nation's founding fathers. 2. This Patriot is known for trying to prove that lightning is electricity.
John Glenn 1. This astronaut was the first American to orbit Earth. 2. This astronaut later became a United States senator.	**Jane Goodall** 1. She is best known for her study of the social behavior of chimpanzees. 2. During her study of chimpanzees, she discovered that they have the ability to make tools.
Nathan Hale 1. He is believed to be America's first spy. 2. When captured, he is believed to have said, "I only regret that I have but one life to lose for my country."	**Alexander Hamilton** 1. He was the first Secretary of the Treasury of the United States. 2. With John Jay and James Madison, he authored the *Federalist Papers,* encouraging ratification of the *Constitution.*

Famous People Bingo

© Barbara M. Peller

Patrick Henry

1. This Patriot from Virginia is known for saying, "Give me liberty, or give me death!"
2. Although he was never President, he did become the first governor of Virginia.

Henry Hudson

1. This English explorer was hired by the Dutch East India Company to find a waterway from Europe to Asia. He sailed on a ship called the *Half Moon.*
2. The large river he explored in what is now New York State is named for him.

Thomas Jefferson

1. He was the first Secretary of State of the United States and the third President of the United States.
2. This Virginia Patriot is credited with writing the rough draft of the *Declaration of Independence.*

Helen Keller

1. Although both deaf and blind, she became a world-famous lecturer.
2. The story of how her teacher, Anne Sullivan, taught her to communicate became the basis for a well-known play, *The Miracle Worker.*

Francis Scott Key

1. He wrote the "Star Spangled Banner."
2. He wrote what became the national anthem of the U.S. during the War of 1812.

Martin Luther King, Jr.

1. This well-known civil-rights leader made his "I Have a Dream" speech on August 28, 1963.
2. This civil-rights leader was assassinated in Memphis, Tennessee, on April 4, 1968.

Marquis de Lafayette

1. This French citizen aided Americans during the American Revolution.
2. One way this Frenchman helped was by getting French land and naval support for the Americans.

Robert E. Lee

1. He was the commander of the Confederate troops during the American Civil War.
2. He surrendered to General Ulysses S. Grant at Appomattox Court House on April 9, 1865.

Meriwether Lewis

1. He was leader of the expedition to explore the lands obtained as a result of the Louisiana Purchase.
2. He asked William Clark to join him as co-leader of the expedition to explore the Louisiana Territory.

Abraham Lincoln

1. This sixteenth President of the United States was President during the Civil War. He was assassinated on April 15, 1865.
2. He is known for both his "Gettysburg Address" and the "Emancipation Proclamation."

© Barbara M. Peller

James Madison	**Ferdinand Magellan**
1. He was the fourth President of the United States. His wife Dolley was a well-liked first lady. 2. He is often called the Father of the United States *Constitution*.	1. This Portuguese explorer was the first to lead an expedition around the world. 2. Although 18 men in his party made it around the world, this explorer did not.
James Monroe	**Florence Nightingale**
1. He was the fifth President of the United States 2. The doctrine named for him was based on advice from John Quincy Adams. It warned Europeans not to interfere in the Americas.	1. This English woman was a pioneer in nursing. 2. She and the nurses she trained helped care for the British soldiers wounded during the Crimean War.
Barack Obama	**Rosa Parks**
1. He became the 44th President of the United States when he assumed office on January 20, 2009. 2. He was the first African-American to be elected President of the United States.	1. She refused to give up her seat on the bus to a white passenger. 2. Her refusal to give up her seat on a bus led to the Montgomery, Alabama, Bus Boycott.
Molly Pitcher	**Pocahontas**
1. This is the nickname of Mary Hays McCauly. 2. She earned this nickname by bringing water to the soldiers during the Battle of Monmouth in New Jersey on June 28, 1778.	1. This Native American woman married an Englishman named John Rolfe. 2. She was the daughter of Powhatan, an Algonquian chief.
Paul Revere	**Betsy Ross**
1. This Boston Patriot was a silversmith. He took part in the Boston Tea Party. 2. Along with William Dawes and Dr. Samuel Prescott, he warned the Patriots at Lexington that the British were coming.	1. She is credited with designing the first American flag. 2. The flag she is credited with designing had the same number of red and white stripes as the modern flag. It had 13 stars.

© Barbara M. Peller

Sacajawea 1. This Shoshone woman and her husband accompanied Lewis and Clark on their famous expedition. 2. She helped Lewis and Clark by acting as interpreter.	**Sequoyah** 1. He invented the Cherokee alphabet. 2. He was a Cherokee warrior.
Dr. Seuss 1. His real name was Theodor Seuss Geisel. He was the author of more than 60 children's books. 2. Two of the many books written by this author are *The Cat in the Hat* and *Green Eggs and Ham.*	**William Shakespeare** 1. He is thought by many to be the greatest writer in the English language. He lived from 1564 to 1616. 2. He wrote *Romeo and Juliet* among many other works.
Mark Twain 1. The real name of this great American author was Samuel Langhorne Clemens. 2. This author is best known for his *Adventures of Tom Sawyer* and *The Adventures of Huckleberry Finn.*	**Harriet Tubman** 1. This abolitionist is best known for her work in the Underground Railroad. At great danger to herself, she helped hundreds of slaves escape. 2. This runaway slave became known as the "Grandma Moses."
Leonardo da Vinci 1. This brilliant Italian was a scientist, inventor, painter, sculptor and mathematician among other things. 2. Two of his most famous paintings are the *Mona Lisa* and *The Last Supper!*	**George Washington** 1. He was commander in chief of the Continental Army. 2. He was the first President of the United States.
Eli Whitney 1. He is known as the inventor of the cotton gin, which made the planting of cotton much more profitable. 2. The machine he invented made it easier to separate the cotton fibers from the seedpods and sticky seeds.	**Wright Brothers** 1. They are credited with building the first successful airplane. They invented the controls that made fixed-wing flight possible. 2. Their names were Orville and Wilbur.

Famous People Bingo

© Barbara M. Peller

Famous People Bingo

Helen Keller	Alexander Hamilton	William Shakespeare	Eli Whitney	Harriet Tubman
Davy Crockett	Abigail Adams	George Washington	James Madison	Thomas Jefferson
Betsy Ross	Molly Pitcher		Martin Luther King, Jr.	James Monroe
Wright Brothers	John Adams	Jane Goodall	Sacajawea	Francis Scott Key
Marquis de Lafayette	Thomas Edison	Roald Dahl	John Glenn	Nathan Hale

© Barbara M. Peller

Famous People Bingo

Wright Brothers	Dr. Seuss	Meriwether Lewis	Florence Nightingale	Marquis de Lafayette
Francis Scott Key	James Madison	Neil Armstrong	John Adams	Paul Revere
Rosa Parks	Thomas Edison		Walt Disney	Jane Goodall
Benjamin Franklin	Sequoyah	Molly Pitcher	Robert E. Lee	Thomas Jefferson
Nathan Hale	George Washington	Roald Dahl	Davy Crockett	John Glenn

© Barbara M. Peller

Famous People Bingo

Wright Brothers	Jane Goodall	James Madison	Sacajawea	Betsy Ross
Thomas Edison	Abigail Adams	Ludwig van Beethoven	Alexander Hamilton	Henry Hudson
John Adams	George Washington		Paul Revere	Susan B. Anthony
Molly Pitcher	Rosa Parks	Marquis de Lafayette	Benjamin Franklin	Meriwether Lewis
John Glenn	Davy Crockett	Roald Dahl	Robert E. Lee	William Shakespeare

Famous People Bingo: Card No. 3

© Barbara M. Peller

Famous People Bingo

Molly Pitcher	Paul Revere	Marquis de Lafayette	Davy Crockett	William Shakespeare
Abraham Lincoln	Neil Armstrong	Alexander Hamilton	Florence Nightingale	Betsy Ross
Martin Luther King, Jr.	Benjamin Franklin		Harriet Tubman	Eli Whitney
Jane Goodall	Pocahontas	George Washington	Roald Dahl	Ludwig van Beethoven
Patrick Henry	Nathan Hale	Ferdinand Magellan	John Glenn	James Monroe

© Barbara M. Peller

Famous People Bingo

Nathan Hale	Harriet Tubman	John Adams	Neil Armstrong	Davy Crockett
Abraham Lincoln	Jane Goodall	Ludwig van Beethoven	Walt Disney	Abigail Adams
Dr. Seuss	James Monroe		Frederick Douglass	Albert Einstein
Thomas Jefferson	Paul Revere	Helen Keller	Robert E. Lee	Patrick Henry
James Madison	Roald Dahl	Pocahontas	Molly Pitcher	Martin Luther King, Jr.

© Barbara M. Peller

Famous People Bingo

Susan B. Anthony	Paul Revere	Meriwether Lewis	Dr. Seuss	James Monroe
Sacajawea	John Adams	Patrick Henry	Alexander Hamilton	Betsy Ross
Florence Nightingale	Ludwig van Beethoven		Neil Armstrong	Walt Disney
Roald Dahl	Marquis de Lafayette	Robert E. Lee	Ferdinand Magellan	William Shakespeare
Francis Scott Key	Jane Goodall	Helen Keller	Martin Luther King, Jr.	Pocahontas

© Barbara M. Peller

Famous People Bingo

Helen Keller	Paul Revere	Albert Einstein	Frederick Douglass	James Madison
Francis Scott Key	William Shakespeare	Thomas Edison	Abigail Adams	Abraham Lincoln
Meriwether Lewis	Eli Whitney		Walt Disney	Clara Barton
Molly Pitcher	Benjamin Franklin	Betsy Ross	Wright Brothers	Rosa Parks
Roald Dahl	Davy Crockett	Robert E. Lee	Ferdinand Magellan	Susan B. Anthony

Famous People Bingo: Card No. 7

© Barbara M. Peller

Famous People Bingo

Martin Luther King, Jr.	Paul Revere	Christopher Columbus	Sacajawea	Clara Barton
Abraham Lincoln	Dr. Seuss	Florence Nightingale	James Monroe	Neil Armstrong
Betsy Ross	Barack Obama		William Shakespeare	Harriet Tubman
John Glenn	Molly Pitcher	Wright Brothers	Patrick Henry	Benjamin Franklin
George Washington	Roald Dahl	Ferdinand Magellan	John Adams	Francis Scott Key

© Barbara M. Peller

Famous People Bingo

Walt Disney	James Madison	Thomas Edison	Betsy Ross	James Monroe
Patrick Henry	Dr. Seuss	Martin Luther King, Jr.	John Adams	William Shakespeare
Henry Hudson	Helen Keller		Abigail Adams	Christopher Columbus
Clara Barton	Nathan Hale	Marquis de Lafayette	Frederick Douglass	Albert Einstein
Benjamin Franklin	Robert E. Lee	Ludwig van Beethoven	Wright Brothers	Harriet Tubman

Famous People Bingo: Card No. 9

© Barbara M. Peller

Famous People Bingo

Wright Brothers	Sacajawea	Neil Armstrong	Florence Nightingale	Pocahontas
James Monroe	Clara Barton	Alexander Hamilton	Abigail Adams	William Shakespeare
Barack Obama	Paul Revere		Eli Whitney	Rosa Parks
Marquis de Lafayette	Thomas Jefferson	Patrick Henry	Robert E. Lee	Henry Hudson
Alexander Graham Bell	Francis Scott Key	Meriwether Lewis	Nathan Hale	Martin Luther King, Jr.

Famous People Bingo: Card No. 10

© Barbara M. Peller

Famous People Bingo

Susan B. Anthony	Paul Revere	John Adams	Patrick Henry	Francis Scott Key
Christopher Columbus	Henry Hudson	Frederick Douglass	Walt Disney	Alexander Hamilton
Abraham Lincoln	Dr. Seuss		Meriwether Lewis	Thomas Edison
Alexander Graham Bell	Betsy Ross	Robert E. Lee	Davy Crockett	Wright Brothers
Ludwig van Beethoven	Roald Dahl	Helen Keller	Ferdinand Magellan	James Madison

© Barbara M. Peller

Famous People Bingo

James Madison	Harriet Tubman	Henry Hudson	Sacajawea	Walt Disney
Thomas Edison	George Washington	Dr. Seuss	Ferdinand Magellan	Abigail Adams
Helen Keller	Albert Einstein		James Monroe	Florence Nightingale
Roald Dahl	Benjamin Franklin	William Shakespeare	Wright Brothers	Abraham Lincoln
Paul Revere	Christopher Columbus	Barack Obama	Ludwig van Beethoven	Clara Barton

© Barbara M. Peller

Famous People Bingo

Alexander Graham Bell	Harriet Tubman	Susan B. Anthony	Henry Hudson	James Monroe
Dr. Seuss	Christopher Columbus	Paul Revere	Walt Disney	Rosa Parks
Sacajawea	Neil Armstrong		Thomas Edison	Albert Einstein
Martin Luther King, Jr.	Robert E. Lee	Clara Barton	Barack Obama	Wright Brothers
Roald Dahl	Thomas Jefferson	Ferdinand Magellan	Helen Keller	Frederick Douglass

Famous People Bingo: Card No.13

© Barbara M. Peller

Famous People Bingo

Davy Crockett	Dr. Seuss	John Adams	Walt Disney	Alexander Graham Bell
Clara Barton	Helen Keller	Henry Hudson	Abigail Adams	Paul Revere
Patrick Henry	Eli Whitney		Meriwether Lewis	Ludwig van Beethoven
Thomas Jefferson	Robert E. Lee	Barack Obama	Neil Armstrong	Susan B. Anthony
Roald Dahl	Florence Nightingale	Rosa Parks	Francis Scott Key	Martin Luther King, Jr.

© Barbara M. Peller

Famous People Bingo

Frederick Douglass	Walt Disney	John Adams	James Madison	Sacajawea
Susan B. Anthony	Meriwether Lewis	Alexander Hamilton	Dr. Seuss	Patrick Henry
James Monroe	Helen Keller		Betsy Ross	William Shakespeare
Roald Dahl	Henry Hudson	Christopher Columbus	Robert E. Lee	Alexander Graham Bell
Francis Scott Key	Benjamin Franklin	Ferdinand Magellan	Pocahontas	Thomas Edison

Famous People Bingo: Card No. 15

© Barbara M. Peller

Famous People Bingo

Neil Armstrong	Henry Hudson	Christopher Columbus	Pocahontas	Sequoyah
Florence Nightingale	Rosa Parks	Albert Einstein	Abraham Lincoln	Eli Whitney
Alexander Graham Bell	Harriet Tubman		James Monroe	Thomas Edison
Molly Pitcher	Clara Barton	Roald Dahl	Frederick Douglass	Wright Brothers
Patrick Henry	Leonardo da Vinci	Ferdinand Magellan	Benjamin Franklin	Paul Revere

Famous People Bingo: Card No. 16

© Barbara M. Peller

Famous People Bingo

Alexander Graham Bell	Mark Twain	Henry Ford	Henry Hudson	Davy Crockett
Frederick Douglass	Patrick Henry	Robert E. Lee	Eli Whitney	Albert Einstein
Walt Disney	Martin Luther King, Jr.		Leonardo da Vinci	Christopher Columbus
Nathan Hale	Francis Scott Key	Wright Brothers	John Adams	Rosa Parks
Marquis de Lafayette	Ludwig van Beethoven	James Madison	Sacajawea	Harriet Tubman

Famous People Bingo: Card No. 17

© Barbara M. Peller

Famous People Bingo

Pocahontas	Barack Obama	Clara Barton	Patrick Henry	Florence Nightingale
Paul Revere	Alexander Graham Bell	Marquis de Lafayette	James Monroe	Ludwig van Beethoven
Walt Disney	Rosa Parks		Henry Ford	William Shakespeare
Nathan Hale	Alexander Hamilton	Robert E. Lee	Wright Brothers	Meriwether Lewis
Leonardo da Vinci	Henry Hudson	John Adams	Mark Twain	Susan B. Anthony

Famous People Bingo: Card No. 18

© Barbara M. Peller

Famous People Bingo

James Monroe	Susan B. Anthony	Henry Hudson	Christopher Columbus	Barack Obama
Frederick Douglass	Sacajawea	William Shakespeare	James Madison	Eli Whitney
Mark Twain	Davy Crockett		Abigail Adams	Pocahontas
Meriwether Lewis	Leonardo da Vinci	Marquis de Lafayette	Benjamin Franklin	Henry Ford
Betsy Ross	Sequoyah	Francis Scott Key	Martin Luther King, Jr.	Ferdinand Magellan

Famous People Bingo: Card No. 19

© Barbara M. Peller

Famous People Bingo

Barack Obama	Mark Twain	Sacajawea	Henry Hudson	Abigail Adams
Neil Armstrong	Thomas Edison	Abraham Lincoln	Marquis de Lafayette	Florence Nightingale
Harriet Tubman	Albert Einstein		Molly Pitcher	Alexander Hamilton
Nathan Hale	George Washington	John Glenn	Benjamin Franklin	Leonardo da Vinci
Jane Goodall	Martin Luther King, Jr.	Sequoyah	Wright Brothers	Henry Ford

Famous People Bingo: Card No. 20

© Barbara M. Peller

Famous People Bingo

Frederick Douglass	Susan B. Anthony	Abraham Lincoln	Henry Hudson	Thomas Jefferson
Harriet Tubman	Henry Ford	Clara Barton	Christopher Columbus	Helen Keller
Rosa Parks	Francis Scott Key		Mark Twain	John Adams
Marquis de Lafayette	James Madison	Leonardo da Vinci	Nathan Hale	Martin Luther King, Jr.
Molly Pitcher	Sequoyah	Ferdinand Magellan	Alexander Graham Bell	Benjamin Franklin

Famous People Bingo: Card No. 21

© Barbara M. Peller

Famous People Bingo

Betsy Ross	Meriwether Lewis	Henry Ford	Dr. Seuss	Alexander Graham Bell
Florence Nightingale	Sacajawea	Pocahontas	Christopher Columbus	Abigail Adams
Clara Barton	Eli Whitney		Helen Keller	Albert Einstein
Leonardo da Vinci	Nathan Hale	Benjamin Franklin	Alexander Hamilton	Davy Crockett
Sequoyah	Ludwig van Beethoven	Mark Twain	Rosa Parks	Abraham Lincoln

© Barbara M. Peller

Famous People Bingo

Neil Armstrong	Mark Twain	James Madison	Dr. Seuss	Ferdinand Magellan
Susan B. Anthony	Barack Obama	Francis Scott Key	Frederick Douglass	Alexander Hamilton
Meriwether Lewis	Alexander Graham Bell		John Glenn	Helen Keller
Rosa Parks	Sequoyah	Leonardo da Vinci	Ludwig van Beethoven	Benjamin Franklin
Thomas Jefferson	George Washington	Martin Luther King, Jr.	Marquis de Lafayette	Henry Ford

Famous People Bingo: Card No. 23

© Barbara M. Peller

Famous People Bingo

Neil Armstrong	Barack Obama	Davy Crockett	Mark Twain	Christopher Columbus
James Monroe	Ferdinand Magellan	Abraham Lincoln	Florence Nightingale	Helen Keller
Albert Einstein	Pocahontas		Alexander Graham Bell	Rosa Parks
Thomas Jefferson	John Glenn	Leonardo da Vinci	Ludwig van Beethoven	Harriet Tubman
Jane Goodall	Molly Pitcher	Sequoyah	Sacajawea	George Washington

© Barbara M. Peller

Famous People Bingo

Molly Pitcher	Abraham Lincoln	Mark Twain	John Adams	Henry Ford
Alexander Hamilton	Thomas Jefferson	Frederick Douglass	Dr. Seuss	Abigail Adams
Harriet Tubman	Christopher Columbus		John Glenn	Leonardo da Vinci
Pocahontas	Nathan Hale	George Washington	Sequoyah	Eli Whitney
Ferdinand Magellan	Davy Crockett	Clara Barton	Patrick Henry	Jane Goodall

© Barbara M. Peller

Famous People Bingo

Henry Ford	Mark Twain	Meriwether Lewis	Florence Nightingale	Pocahontas
Marquis de Lafayette	Sacajawea	Christopher Columbus	Barack Obama	Neil Armstrong
Thomas Jefferson	John Glenn		Eli Whitney	Molly Pitcher
Alexander Graham Bell	Dr. Seuss	Nathan Hale	Sequoyah	Leonardo da Vinci
Albert Einstein	Patrick Henry	John Adams	George Washington	Jane Goodall

© Barbara M. Peller

Famous People Bingo

Meriwether Lewis	Clara Barton	Mark Twain	Barack Obama	Thomas Edison
Thomas Jefferson	John Glenn	Frederick Douglass	Leonardo da Vinci	Abigail Adams
Robert E. Lee	George Washington		Sequoyah	Molly Pitcher
Pocahontas	Susan B. Anthony	Abraham Lincoln	Jane Goodall	Alexander Hamilton
Alexander Graham Bell	Eli Whitney	Henry Ford	Betsy Ross	Albert Einstein

Famous People Bingo: Card No. 27

© Barbara M. Peller

Famous People Bingo

James Monroe	Barack Obama	Pocahontas	Mark Twain	Clara Barton
Thomas Edison	Henry Ford	John Glenn	Florence Nightingale	Eli Whitney
George Washington	Rosa Parks		Albert Einstein	Marquis de Lafayette
Wright Brothers	Betsy Ross	Francis Scott Key	Sequoyah	Leonardo da Vinci
Dr. Seuss	Walt Disney	Alexander Graham Bell	Jane Goodall	Thomas Jefferson

© Barbara M. Peller

Famous People Bingo

Henry Ford	Barack Obama	Pocahontas	Frederick Douglass	Walt Disney
Thomas Jefferson	Marquis de Lafayette	Abraham Lincoln	Albert Einstein	Betsy Ross
Harriet Tubman	John Glenn		Abigail Adams	Mark Twain
Thomas Edison	Nathan Hale	William Shakespeare	Sequoyah	Leonardo da Vinci
Neil Armstrong	Christopher Columbus	Jane Goodall	Susan B. Anthony	George Washington

Famous People Bingo: Card No. 29

© Barbara M. Peller

Famous People Bingo

Davy Crockett	Mark Twain	Florence Nightingale	Walt Disney	Leonardo da Vinci
Alexander Hamilton	Barack Obama	Meriwether Lewis	Eli Whitney	Abigail Adams
Thomas Jefferson	Alexander Graham Bell		Albert Einstein	Abraham Lincoln
Jane Goodall	Susan B. Anthony	William Shakespeare	Sequoyah	John Glenn
Nathan Hale	James Madison	George Washington	Henry Ford	Pocahontas

Famous People Bingo: Card No. 30

© Barbara M. Peller

www.ingramcontent.com/pod-product-compliance
Lightning Source LLC
LaVergne TN
LVHW061337060426
835511LV00014B/1973